What is a Savior?

The True Story of God's Daring Plan to Rescue Us

Written by
Jennifer Kimbrell

Illustrated by
Kayla Almon

Thanks to obsidiandawn.com for the Photoshop brushes used in the illustrations.

Thanks to Mrs. Jill Brandon, Mrs. Laurie Cordaro, Miss Grace Cornelison, Mrs. Wendy Cornelison, Mrs. Carol Gilmore, Mrs. Cathy Haynie, and Dr. John Kwasny for taking time to review the book and suggest improvements.

Thanks to Dr. J. B. Webster and Mr. Andrew Pudewa for the *Institute for Excellence in Writing* method.

Thanks to Dr. John W. P. Oliver and Dr. Gordon K. Reed for the years of faithful, fruitful preaching of the Word.

Dear Readers,

The Bible is the thrilling, true story of God's heroic rescue of people in terrible danger. Although there are many fascinating people in Bible events, God is the champion of the epic. Throughout the Bible, God proves over and over that He is a God who saves!

This book tells "the old, old story of Jesus and His love." Still, as our beloved pastor Dr. Gordon Reed often reminded us, "God's words are the ONLY words He has ever PROMISED to bless!" God's Word, the Bible, is living and powerful. After reading this book, take time to read the whole story in God's own words! He PROMISES He will bless them!

With joy,
Jennifer and Kayla

Where to find the Bible stories in your Bible:

The Story of Noah: Genesis 6—9:17

The Story of Joseph: Genesis 37—46

The Story of Moses: Exodus 2—15:21

The Story of Rahab: Joshua 2, 6

The Story of David and Goliath: 1 Samuel 17

The Story of Jonah: The Book of Jonah

The Story of Daniel in the Lions' Den: Daniel 6

The Story of Esther: The Book of Esther

The Story of Adam and Eve: Genesis 1—4

The Story of Jesus: The Books of Matthew, Mark, Luke and John

The Bible tells us that Jesus is our Savior.

But . . .

WHAT is a SAVIOR?

A savior saves people who are in terrible danger. A savior rescues them. The Bible tells the amazing, true story of how God saved people who were in terrible danger.

Our God is a God who saves!
The Sovereign Lord rescues us from death.
Psalm 68:20

One of those people was Noah. When he lived, most people were horribly wicked. This made God angry and sad. He was sorry He had created them. To wash the world clean, God planned a huge flood over the whole earth. Although Noah worshipped and obeyed God, he was in danger from that flood, too.

Lovingly, God warned Noah about the flood ahead of time. God explained how to build a sturdy boat that would protect him. Noah listened and obeyed. He carefully followed all of God's instructions. When the ferocious flood burst upon the earth, God saved Noah and his family by keeping them safe inside the boat.

God waited patiently while Noah was building his boat.
Only eight people were saved from drowning in that terrible flood.
1 Peter 3:20b

Many years after the flood there lived a huge family named Israel. God had chosen them as His special people. One of the youngest boys, Joseph, had ten older brothers! Sadly, they were jealous of Joseph. After kidnapping him, they sold him as a slave. Joseph was carried far away to Egypt.

In Egypt, God took care of Joseph. God also warned him about a coming famine, a long time with no food. He directed Joseph to save up grain ahead of time so there would be plenty later. When Joseph's huge, hungry family was in danger of starving, they trudged to Egypt, searching for food. God saved the whole family with the grain Joseph had collected.

"God has sent me ahead of you to keep you and your families alive and to save you with an extraordinary rescue."
Genesis 45:7

Because Joseph had been so helpful in Egypt, the king gave his family some of the best land as their home. They lived there for many years. Then a boy named Moses was born. By that time, the generous king had died. A cruel king ruled instead. Harshly, he forced Israel to work as slaves! They cried to God for help.

When Moses grew old, God chose him as the leader of Israel. Moses led God's people out of Egypt. Angrily, the Egyptian king raced after them with his army. His slaves were escaping! Reaching the seashore, Moses and his relatives were trapped between the deep water and the dangerous soldiers. God saved them by making a path through the sea so they could escape.

But Moses told the people, "Don't be afraid.
Just stand still and watch the LORD rescue you today."
Exodus 14:13a

Moses led them toward a new land that God had promised them. The people complained and quarreled constantly. Although God had taken such good care of them, they still didn't trust Him! This made God very unhappy. They wandered in the desert for forty years before He finally allowed them to enter the new land.

A woman named Rahab lived there in the city of Jericho. She had heard of Israel and believed in their God. When some spies from Israel arrived, Rahab helped them. Knowing the city was in danger from Israel's army, she asked the spies to protect her. God saved Rahab and her whole family by sending the spies to rescue them from Jericho.

The men who had been spies went in and brought out Rahab…
They moved her whole family to a safe place near the camp of Israel.
Joshua 6:23

God's people settled in the new land, which they called "Israel," just like their family name. In Israel they battled lots of enemies who did not want them there. During one war, they were in danger from a huge, cruel soldier named Goliath. He yelled wicked things about God. He dared Israel's army to fight him. He bragged that he would beat their best soldier and make them all slaves. Israel's army was too afraid to fight.

One day, a young man named David visited the army camp. When he heard about Goliath's brutal plans, David knew the evil man had to be stopped. David was a shepherd, not a soldier, but God saved His people by helping David kill Goliath.

"The LORD who rescued me from the claws of the lion and the bear will rescue me from this Philistine!"
1 Samuel 17:37a

Later, God sent a man named Jonah to visit some of Israel's enemies. Because God cared about them, He wanted Jonah to warn them. These enemies were horribly wicked and cruel. They hated God's people. Jonah did not want to help them. Foolishly, he tried to escape from God by sailing away in a ship.

While Jonah was at sea, God sent a savage storm to stop him. Jonah finally told the sailors that the storm was his fault, because he was running away from God. The men were shocked and scared. At last, they threw Jonah overboard, and the storm stopped. Jonah was in danger of drowning! God saved him by sending a gigantic fish to swallow him and take him back to land.

Jonah said, "I cried out to the LORD in my great trouble, and he answered me. I called to you from the land of the dead, and LORD, you heard me!"
Jonah 2:2

After a while, Israel began to ignore God. They disobeyed Him. Although God warned them again and again, still they would not listen! Finally, a fierce army attacked. They captured many of God's people, including a young man named Daniel. The prisoners were carried far away to their enemies' strange land.

There, the king signed an awful new law. He promised that anyone who prayed to God would be fed to the lions! Knowing that God's law was more important than the king's, Daniel prayed anyway. He was caught and thrown into the lions' den. Daniel was in great danger from the hungry lions, but God saved him by sending an angel to shut their mouths.

"My God sent His angel and shut the lions' mouths
so that they would not hurt me..."
Daniel 6:22

After many years, God's people were allowed to return to Israel. Since the strange land of Persia had been their home for such a long time, some of them would not leave. A man named Mordecai stayed. He cared for his orphan cousin, Esther, like a daughter. Amazingly, when the Persian king needed a new queen, he chose beautiful Esther! No one knew she was from Israel.

Haman, one of the Persians, hated Mordecai and the rest of God's people. Wickedly, Haman plotted to destroy them. They were in serious danger. Although Esther was afraid, God gave her courage to go boldly to the king to ask for his help. God saved His people by directing the king to help them.

So let us come boldly to the throne of our gracious God. There we will receive his mercy, and we will find grace to help us when we need it most.
Hebrews 4:16

All of these people were in terrible danger and God saved them. He was their Savior.

But . . .

Why do WE need a Savior?
What kind of danger are WE in?

That part of the story began a long time ago, before we were born, before Jesus was born, before Esther, Daniel, Jonah, David, Rahab, Moses, Joseph, or even Noah were born.

God decided in advance to adopt us into his own family
by bringing us to himself through Jesus Christ.
This is what he wanted to do, and it gave him great pleasure.
Ephesians 1:5

God created a beautiful world. Everything was perfect! He even planted a special garden filled with wonderful fruit trees. When God finally finished His world, He made the first people, Adam and Eve. They were perfect, too, because they were made like God. Their hearts were good, like His, so they could obey Him. God was very pleased with them. He was their friend.

Since God was with them, Adam and Eve were happy and safe in their beautiful garden home. They could walk and talk with God. He explained that they could eat fruit from any of the garden's lovely trees, except for one special tree. From that tree they could not eat. God promised they would die if they disobeyed.

But the Lord God warned him…"If you eat its fruit, you are sure to die."
Genesis 2:16a, 17b

Adam and Eve could choose to obey and please God, because their hearts were good like His. They could also choose to disobey. Did they obey? No! They disobeyed God and ate the fruit anyway. Disobeying God is what the Bible calls "sin."

Next, the most terrible thing happened. Once they disobeyed God, their hearts became sinful through and through. They were not good like God anymore.

When Adam sinned, sin entered the world.
Romans 5:12a

God hates sin. He will only live with people who are good like Him. He won't live with people who have sinful hearts, so Adam and Eve could no longer live with God. They had to leave their garden home. When they were good, they had been happy and safe. Now, Adam and Eve were sinful, unhappy and lonely.

Their friendship with God changed, too. Instead of wanting to please Him, now they cared about pleasing themselves! Instead of obeying God, now they constantly disobeyed Him. Even worse, instead of enjoying God, now they were afraid of Him.

Your eyes are too pure to look on evil;
you cannot tolerate wrong.
Habakkuk 1:13a

Adam and Eve didn't die right away. When their first baby was born, they named him Cain. The next son they called Abel. The boys probably looked a lot like their mom and dad. They talked just like their mom and dad. Sadly, they also had sinful hearts like their mom and dad, so they disobeyed God, too.

Cain was jealous of Abel. One day when they were grown up, Cain grew so angry with his brother that he killed him. Then Adam and Eve understood what God meant when He warned them that they would die.

For the wages of sin is death,
but the free gift of God is eternal life through Christ Jesus our Lord.
Romans 6:23

Adam and Eve's other children grew up and had children, and those children grew up and had children, and those children grew up and had children. Like Adam and Eve, all of those children had sinful hearts and disobeyed God.

Finally, just like God promised, they all died. Death is the punishment for disobeying God.

Adam's sin brought death,
so death spread to everyone, for everyone sinned.
Romans 5:12b

Even now, all people are born with sinful hearts. Everyone disobeys God. Sometimes we disobey Him by doing things He says not to do, like lying or stealing. Sometimes we disobey Him by not doing something He wants us to do, like being kind or obeying our parents. Even when we try to obey God we still disobey Him, because we have sinful hearts just like Adam and Eve.

That's why we are in terrible danger. God still hates sin. His home, heaven, is only for people who are good like Him. With our sinful hearts we can't live with God in heaven. Instead of being happy and safe, we will be unhappy and lonely forever.

For everyone has sinned; we all fall short of God's glorious standard.
Romans 3:23

But...

God loves people. He wants people at home in heaven with Him!

He made a plan to save us from our sin. He sent His very own Son, Jesus, to be our Savior. Since Jesus is God's Son, He wasn't born with a sinful heart like Adam's. His heart was good, just like His Father's heart. It didn't have even one tiny bit of sin in it, so Jesus could love, obey, and please God.

"And she will have a son, and you are to name him Jesus,
for he will save his people from their sins."
Matthew 1:21

How did Jesus save us? First, He lived for us. He lived exactly like God wants you and me to live. Because He loved His Father, Jesus always obeyed and pleased Him. You and I can't live that way, because we have sinful hearts. But Jesus could, so He did it for us.

Still, there was one more thing Jesus had to do to save us. He had to take our punishment that God had promised us for disobeying Him. He had to die. When Jesus died on the cross, He did it to take our punishment for our sin.

For God made Christ, who never sinned, to be the offering for our sin,
so that we could be made right with God through Christ.
2 Corinthians 5:21

God allowed Jesus to suffer the horrible punishment in our place. After Jesus died, His friends laid His body in a tomb made of rock. They thought He was gone forever.

But…

On the third day, the most wonderful, surprising thing happened! Jesus came back to life! By raising Jesus from the dead, God showed that He was very pleased with Jesus' life and death for us. The punishment was finished. Jesus had beaten sin! Now people could be saved.

If you confess with your mouth that Jesus is Lord and believe in your heart
that God raised him from the dead, you will be saved…
For "Everyone who calls on the name of the LORD will be saved."
Romans 10:9,13

When God saves people, He does everything that is needed to rescue them! He warns them of the danger from their sinful hearts. He convinces them that Jesus died for them and rose again. He teaches them that Jesus loves them and wants to save them! He even gives them the faith they need to depend on Jesus.

That is not all! Because Jesus already took their punishment, God treats them like they have never even sinned. He also gives them new, good hearts like His so they can love, obey and please Him. God promises that everyone who has this brand new heart will one day live with Him in His home in heaven!

God saved you by his grace when you believed. And you can't take credit for this; it is a gift from God. Salvation is not a reward for the good things we have done, so none of us can boast about it.
Ephesians 2:8-9

We were in terrible danger because of our sin. We couldn't live with God because of our sinful hearts. God saved us by sending Jesus to take the punishment for our sin.

Jesus never sinned, but He died for sinners that He might bring us safely home to God.*

He is our Savior!

Jesus never sinned, but He died for sinners
that He might bring us safely home to God.
1 Peter 3:18*

Jesus can be your Savior, too!

Who is good?
As the Scriptures say, "No one is righteous—not even one." Romans 3:10

Who has sinned?
For everyone has sinned; we all fall short of God's glorious standard. Romans 3:23

Where did sin come from?
When Adam sinned, sin entered the world. Romans 5:12a

What is God's punishment for sin?
For the wages of sin is death... Romans 6:23a

Who took the punishment?
But God showed his great love for us
by sending Christ to die for us while we were still sinners. Romans 5:8

How can I be saved?
If we say we have no sin, we are only fooling ourselves
and refusing to accept the truth. But if we confess our sins to him,
he is faithful and just to forgive us and to cleanse us from every wrong. 1 John 1:8—9

If you confess with your mouth that Jesus is Lord
and believe in your heart that God raised him from the dead, you will be saved...
For "Everyone who calls on the name of the LORD will be saved." Romans 10:9, 13

What does God promise?
...but the free gift of God is eternal life through Christ Jesus our Lord.
Romans 6:23b

If you have trusted Jesus as your Savior we would love to hear from you.
If you have questions about how to know that Jesus is your Savior,
we would be glad to talk to you.
If you would like to order multiple copies of this book
to use for evangelism, we can provide them at our cost.

Please e-mail us at:
whatisasavior@gmail.com

For more information about this book and about following Jesus,
visit our Facebook page listed as
What is a Savior?